Kayaking
RIDING THE RAPIDS

by Sarah B. Beurskens

Perfection Learning®

Cover Photo: Yampa River kayaker courtesy of Joe Rife
Inside Illustration: Randy Messer
Photographs courtesy of Joe Rife: pp 4, 23, 37, 38, 52, 53, 54.

About the Author

Sarah Beurskens lives in a cabin in Steamboat Springs, Colorado, with her husband Mike and five-year-old black lab Bailey. Her hobbies include downhill skiing, hiking, mountain biking, foreign traveling, reading a good book on a cold winter day, tubing the Yampa River on a warm summer day, and most recently kayaking.

Unfortunately, she doesn't get to go kayaking as much as she'd like to. Her dog Bailey loves the water but hasn't learned to kayak. Ms. Beurskens hopes that someday Bailey will learn the fine skill of balancing on top of a kayak so they can slice through the water together.

Table of Contents

Introduction

Dear Readers,

Kayaking is an exciting sport. It takes you right to the river's edge. You slice through thundering rapids. What a thrill!

However, kayaking can be dangerous. So don't attempt it without a trained instructor. Even skilled paddlers get into scary situations.

In this book, I share the adventures of some friends of mine. All the stories are true.

Read these stories in any order you like. But don't let these adventures scare you. Remember, as a beginning kayaker, you won't start in high-level rapids.

You can read about learning to kayak in "Beginner Blunder" starting on page 27. It's my own story. And if I can kayak, you can too.

I hope you enjoy reading these stories as much as I enjoyed writing them.

Best regards,

Sarah Beurskens

Chapter 1

A Scare in Tunnel Falls

The **put-in** at Gore Canyon was pretty much like the last two times he'd kayaked this section of the Colorado River. Except that this time it was about 40 degrees colder.

It was the Saturday following Thanksgiving. And with the temperature at 35 degrees, Ben Coleman was dancing around to keep from freezing. He was with three of his friends. They were all good kayakers who had also done this section of the Colorado before.

They were ready for a great day on the river. They saw flat water as far as the eye could see. But downriver, **Class IV and V+** rapids awaited them. And they couldn't wait to get there.

Class I   Beginner's water. Waves are ripples. The current is slow to moderate.

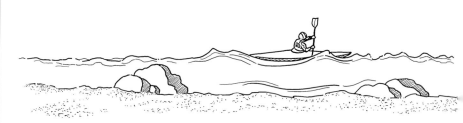

Class II   Basic white-water skill needed. Waves are up to one foot high. Faster current. The course of the river is easy to see.

Class III   Good white-water skills needed. Waves are up to three feet. Fast current. The course of the river is passable. But it needs to be checked for boulders and holes. Class III is the limit for open boats.

Class IV   Advanced to expert skill required. Huge waves. Very fast current. Needs careful inspection.

Class V   Expert skills are a must! Raging, pounding waves. Violent rapids. This level is almost too dangerous to be fun.

DON'T

Class VI   Even experts usually avoid this water. Navigating this level is almost impossible.

The water was ice-cold as they put their kayaks in. It was an easy go on the flat water at the start. So this gave the four kayakers time to gaze at the canyon. Powerful red walls rose straight out of the water. The walls rose up toward the sky until they leveled off into a **mesa.**

Ben looked from side to side. On the left, the cliff walls sliced a sharp path straight into the current. The train track followed the river on the right.

A train shuttled passengers from all over the country. Many had never seen white-water rafters before. Especially on a Thanksgiving weekend.

Because of the tall cliff walls, the sun couldn't get inside to the river below. And on this November day, the sun's peak was lower in the sky than in summer. So it seemed especially gloomy.

Ben marveled at the odd lighting in the canyon. This lighting is weird, almost mysterious, Ben thought.

Ben's black and red Perception kayak sliced through the grey waters. The river was running moderately fast at 1,000 **cfs.**

For four miles, the group had paddled mainly flat water. But Gore Rapid, one of the trickiest rapids on the river, loomed ahead.

Gore Rapid was a Class V rapid with a series of three drops. But that wasn't all. Right in the middle was a huge boulder called Decision Rock.

Boaters have a tough choice at Decision Rock. And only seconds to decide. They can go right or left.

Turning left, they go through a huge hole. And if they choose right, they can't change their minds. Trying to change midway can be deadly. The river will pin a boat right up against the rock. The force of the river will press against it.

As Ben approached, he could see a distinct horizon line. To a kayaker, that signals a drop-off.

The speed of the river increased. As Ben hit the rapid, he dropped five feet into a **hole**.

He exited the hole. But immediately ahead of him was Decision Rock. Ben had only a second to make his choice. He chose left.

It turned out to be the smart choice. Ben's boat sliced through the water. And he exited the rapid. He felt relief and joy at the same time. Behind him, his friends came through the rapid cleanly.

Right after Gore Rapid, the sky turned cloudy. Then it started to snow. Now the kayakers had to deal with snow slapping their faces.

The river raced toward Tunnel Falls. It was getting narrower and trickier. The same amount of water was being forced through a smaller opening. So the water's power was increasing as well.

Tunnel Falls was a waterfall with a 12-foot drop-off. On the left side, a rock stuck out, but water passed underneath it. Since it was underwater, kayakers couldn't see the undercut area. The current there could suck them under. And on the right, the landing under the falls was shallow.

The group **eddied out** before the falls. Ben and two of his friends walked downriver to the exit of the falls. They would act as the safety crew for the other boaters.

The crew had orange safety ropes and red **throw bags.** They were ready to toss them to troubled kayakers.

The first three kayakers went through safely. Then they took Ben's place with throw bags in hand.

Now it was Ben's turn. He walked back and climbed into his kayak.

Ben wasn't worried. He'd done this before. He knew the layout of the river and what to watch out for. He knew where he needed to enter the falls to get the proper exit. No worries.

On his **peel out,** Ben did a few power strokes. Just to get his speed up.

On his final stroke, his paddle caught on something. It was yanked out of his hand. His body was jerked hard to the right. Ben dropped over the edge of the falls and into the hole.

The force of the river cartwheeled him. His kayak flipped end over end in the icy water.

Ben had a **scullcap** on. Still the freezing water slammed against his face. It rushed into his mouth. The roar of the river deadened his ears.

Ben's friends yelled at him from the edges. But he couldn't hear them. Nor could he see the three red throw bags. They had been tossed into the river for his rescue.

Ben missed his paddle. He needed it for leverage to do his roll. Once he thought he felt his paddle go by him while he was

underwater. But he couldn't be sure. It could've been a log or something else.

Ben would have to rely on his **handroll.** Luckily, he'd learned it last summer.

Ben stuck his right arm out straight. He flattened his hand for the handroll. He swung his arm up and back hard. For the first time in what seemed like hours, Ben was above water. And he was out of the hole.

He looked around, dazed. He really hadn't been afraid until now. Fear washed rapidly through his body. He was choking. Soon a throbbing ache gripped the front of his face. Like when you eat ice cream too fast.

He eddied out downriver. The others rushed to his side. "Hey, are you okay? Man, what a run!"

Half of the 11-mile trip remained. But Ben was relieved. The worst was behind him.

It was still snowing when Ben pulled his kayak out at the pump house. He glanced back at the mighty river. What a trip! he thought. He hoisted the boat onto his shoulder and climbed up to the car.

Ben and his father built their own kayak. They found a man in California with a kayak mold. Even though it was a 1986 design, they decided to give it a try.

Fiberglass comes in sheets like yards of fabric. Ben and his father placed lengths of it along the mold. Next, they painted a hardener called resin on top of the fiberglass. After the resin dried, they repeated the process.

Ben and his dad laid six layers on the deck (top) of the boat and seven layers on the bottom. They hope to use their boat soon.

Chapter 2

Grand Canyon Glory

"Finally!" Sandy sighed. She had been waiting for five years. It had taken that long to get the permit to run the Grand Canyon.

Permits are required for private launches. And only one private launch per day is allowed. Thousands of people apply. So it takes a while to get to the top of the list.

But the permit wasn't the hardest part for Sandy. Organizing the 20-day trip was harder. She made dozens of calls to gather people, equipment, and food.

At first, people had been excited. But as the day grew closer, problems surfaced. People backed out. That meant more scrambling to get enough people. And worse yet, Sandy was scheduled to make the first evening meal.

The night before their big journey, they set up camp right outside of Lees Ferry. It was near the entrance to the Canyon.

Two of the kayakers couldn't wait to try out the river. So they decided to take a quick cruise that night. A police officer stopped them. They shouldn't have been boating without a permit.

Lees Ferry

Marble
Canyon

Badger
Creek
Rapids

Colorado
River

Lava Falls
Rapids

Grand Canyon
National Park

Diamond
Creek

The Grand Canyon patrol has to be very strict. They have to protect the environment from overuse. So only a limited number of people are allowed on the river each year.

The officer was angry with Sandy too. She was the one responsible for the permit.

As punishment, Sandy put the two kayakers in charge of the groover, the portable toilet. Punishment enough, Sandy thought with a slight chuckle.

But that was all behind her now. Sandy sighed and leaned back in her kayak. She was finally on the river. The Colorado River in the mighty Grand Canyon. What an amazing sight.

Sandy gazed up at the subtle colors of the layered canyon walls. First cream, then buff, white, red, and maroon. The layers rising 2,500 feet to the towering rim.

She entered Marble Canyon. It was a narrow gorge 61 miles long. The canyon walls were so polished they looked like marble.

The hot sun warmed Sandy. The calm water soothed her nerves. She was finally able to relax.

If only these walls could talk, she thought. What amazing stories of adventure they'd reveal!

Canyon History

The Canyon would talk of Spaniards, Anasazi Indians, and white men who had come before. All of them awed by the deep Canyon and the river snaking below its steep rims.

The Canyon would sing the triumph of Major John Powell. He had been the one-armed leader of the first Colorado River expedition in 1869. He and his party faced many challenges. They didn't know what lay ahead of them. Would there be powerful rapids? tumbling waterfalls? Either could be a human deathtrap.

Three men from Major Powell's party had died. But not in the river.

It had been toward the end of the Canyon. They had refused to face the raging rapids. Climbing out of the Canyon, they had been killed by Indians.

But the rest of the party was successful. They traveled the entire length of the Grand Canyon.

Narrow passes would echo the tale of the Mountain Meadows Massacre of 1857. During the massacre, Mormons and Indians killed over 100 people traveling to California.

John Doyle Lee was a key person in the massacre. He later faced a firing squad. Lees Ferry was named in memory of him.

Major John Powell and members of his party during the first Colorado River expedition in 1869.

LOC

Sandy's party consisted of 12 people in 4 rafts and 6 kayaks. Sandy had borrowed a kayak. It was a new yellow Laser kayak straight from the factory.

There were 227 miles and 200 rapids between them and the **take out.**

At mile marker 7, the group began to hear the distant rumbling of Badger Creek Rapids. They eddied out and walked up to observe the rapid.

As they approached, the rasping sound of the river became louder. It was thunderous.

The kayakers peered at the boiling water. It dropped 15 feet over a series of large boulders. Some were as big as 15 feet in diameter.

Major Powell had carried his boats around this rapid. But Sandy and the others decided to run it.

The kayakers walked back and got into their boats. The thought of the first big rapid excited Sandy.

Sandy focused on her goal. She dug her paddle deep into the water. Stroking rapidly, but with control, she sliced through the exploding waves.

Within moments, she emerged safely on the other side. Five minutes later, all boats were through Badger Creek Rapids.

The rafts were loaded with food, tents, and clothing for all 20 days. Sandy worried now that she hadn't packed enough for 12 people. She didn't want to run out of food or supplies. There was nowhere to go for more. They were stuck with what they had until they left the Canyon.

The kayakers were fast approaching House Rock. Here water poured over a house-sized boulder in the middle of the river. This wasn't a well-known rapid. So Sandy's group didn't bother getting out to inspect it.

Earlier, Sandy and the group had joked about which raft would flip first. They had formed a money pool. Each person had put in five dollars. Each had guessed the rapid and the raft that would have the first flip.

Fred was one of the raft guides. He was sure it wouldn't be his raft. In all his years of rafting, he had never flipped. He signed his permit "No Flip" Fred. And no one had bet on House Rock.

The kayakers checked to make sure their gear was tied down. Then they went in and ran it clean.

Fred followed. His passenger, Pat, sat toward the front on top of the gear. The kayakers watched from a sandy beach nearby.

Sandy knew what Fred would have to do. He needed to paddle hard to **river right.** That would get him into the main current of the river. Then the river would guide him cleanly through the hole. She relaxed and watched.

But Fred's raft sped directly over the top of the rock. It spilled over the ledge, dumping Pat, Fred, and everything. "No Flip" Fred had flipped!

First one head popped up. Then another. Okay, they're accounted for, thought Sandy. Now let's save the boat.

The others scrambled out of their kayaks to help retrieve supplies. Luckily, the raft had been spit into an **eddy.** But it was upside down. So the group had to figure out a way to flip the raft over.

The **dry bags** were tightly secured to the raft. So they hadn't floated away. But was everything dry? They'd have to wait until they set up camp to find out.

That night after setting up camp, it was time to check their supplies. Sandy and her group unloaded the dry bags to see what could be saved. Tents, sleeping bags, clothing, and food

emerged. Everything looked good. Warm and dry.

Only one bag of charcoal was wet. Not a bad tally. They could deal with soggy charcoal.

Glen Canyon Dam was located just above Lees Ferry. The dam controlled the release of water. The release of water from the dam produced power. That power traveled over lines to major cities.

During the hot daylight hours, cities needed air conditioning. So great amounts of water were released. At night when it was cooler, the volume was decreased.

This created a problem for paddlers. They pulled their boats onto dry land at night. In the morning, they'd awaken to find the boats floating in the middle of the river. The changing tides on the Colorado tricked Sandy's crew many times.

Serious injuries can occur for boaters in the Canyon. The group's most common injuries, though, were to their toes.

Sandy figured that almost half of the toes on the journey had suffered some damage. They were bitten by red ants, broken while mud sliding, or scraped while going barefoot.

It was their fourteenth day out, and everything had gone surprisingly well. Except for Fred. "No Flip" had capsized again in Lava Rapids.

The whole group pulled their kayaks ashore at Matkatamiba Canyon. They enjoyed a hearty lunch of crab salad. The warm, sunny day was perfect for a hike. So they decided to take half an hour or so to explore a side canyon.

The hike was beautiful. A clear, freshwater stream trickled beside slick, flat rock. Blue pools of water beckoned them to jump in.

But the half-hour hike turned into a two-hour journey. Doc rushed up to Sandy as the hikers returned. "Two kayaks are gone!" he called.

"What?" she cried.

"There are four down there," he said. "And there are supposed to be six."

A million things went through Sandy's head as she rushed down to the water. No kayak. Six days left. How will I get to the take out? Raft? No way! This can't happen. It's not even my kayak. A brand new loaner kayak—gone!

The river had been running between 15,000 to 20,000 cfs on this trip. Sandy grabbed someone else's kayak. She shot out of the eddy and paddled as fast as she could.

Up ahead was Upset Rapid. Normally, she'd have checked it out first and planned her course. But she'd sidestepped that routine. She was in a hurry to find her loaner kayak.

Sandy paddled full tilt toward the rapid. She saw the horizon line. There the river just drops out below.

As Sandy came upon it, she saw its huge size. One giant wave erupted in front of her. Another one surged immediately to the right. She back-paddled hard, but it was too late. She was sucked into it.

The force of the rapid knocked her over. She wrestled with the water briefly before rolling up. She caught her breath and was under again. Another roll. As she came up, the river violently spit her out.

Sandy looked up and saw an eddy. The sight of the calm, peaceful water was a welcome sight. But seeing the two escaped kayaks really thrilled her! There they were, rocking gently in the eddy.

Doc and the others were not far behind. They skillfully ran Upset Rapid. They came around the corner to find the kayaks and Sandy.

Doc was relieved that his 35mm waterproof camera was still sitting in the cockpit. His kayak had managed to stay upright through the rapid.

That night, the crew played guitar and sang. They toasted the successful recovery of the kayaks. And they watched for ringtails.

Ringtails look slightly like raccoons. And they are only found in the Grand Canyon. On previous nights, the creatures had sneaked into the campsite. In the morning, the campers discovered that all their Reese's Peanut Butter Cups had been unwrapped and eaten. So tonight, they were on their guard.

The night was still except for the gentle lapping of the water. Beyond the black-outlined canyon rims, the stars burned. They looked like white diamonds on black velvet.

Each portion of the trip thus far had been a discovery. Each day presented new landscapes, geography, and wildlife.

A feeling of peace settled on Sandy. Sleep had come easily every other night. And she knew it would again tonight.

The last day had finally arrived. Sandy and the others approached Diamond Creek, the take out. She felt proud. They'd done it! The Grand Canyon! What an experience!

But there was a sadness too. It was over. They had to leave. Had Powell and his men felt this way?

Sandy carved her kayak into an eddy. Slowly, she raised herself out. What a trip, she thought. She pulled her boat out of the Colorado River and headed home.

Chapter 3

Beginner Blunder

One day, I decided to try kayaking. I'm not sure why. I guess watching kayakers made me want to try it. Who wouldn't after seeing them paddle with ease along the beautiful blue rivers in the Rockies?

Or was it the thought of hurtling myself through subfreezing water? Water that was snow just yesterday.

So I went to a local kayaking shop. It was well known. It also happened to have the cheapest lessons in town. So naturally, I chose it!

Choosing a kayak was my first task. It's very important to pick out the right boat.

I knew I needed to choose something stable. Something that would support my weight and still float. An aircraft carrier was my first choice. Seeing none, I chose the Wave Sport Extreme.

Four other people took a kayaking lesson with me. Our instructor was called Gator. Gator was in his twenties. He looked like a Grateful Dead groupie. He was balding with little tufts of hair popping out. It worried me that he didn't look very alert. Oftentimes, he looked like a basset hound in the shade.

Gator loaded our boats on the van. We hopped in and rode upriver.

Gator wanted us to practice in calm water. So we pulled into an area near a pond. And the water was calm. So calm, it had a layer of scum on top.

We weren't ready for rapid water. You know, the kind that hurtles humans onto rocks.

Gator hopped on top of the van to unload the kayaks. His bald head was gleaming in the sunshine. We stood below, waiting to grab our boats. I figured the weight of the kayak in relation to the pull of gravity. Then I estimated the rate of descent.

Finally, I decided the best way to get the kayak to the ground was to let it drop. And that's what I did. In one loud boom. One very loud boom. The kayak crashed to the ground.

It was so loud that Gator, the people in my group, the fishermen on the pond, people driving on the highway, bears in the mountains, and the governor in Denver turned to look!

Gator gave me an angry look. And that's how I learned the First Rule of Kayaking Safety.

Always bring donuts to the first lesson!

Donuts are the key. Remember, your instructor holds your life in his hands. So it's important to stay on his good side.

Your life may be precious to you. But not to him. Offering him donuts makes you a little more valuable.

Next, I had to get outfitted. First and foremost, the helmet.

Rocks lie just beneath the surface of the water. When you flip over in a kayak, the force of the water moves your body at high speeds. (Even a Chris Farley-like body!) The force of the water can drive you headfirst into a rock. So a helmet is very important.

28

Next, I needed a **wet suit.** It took a long time to get it on. I was a little worried. As hard as it was to get on, I was sure I'd never get it off again. It was so tight, it seemed to BECOME part of my body. I was sure it would have to be surgically removed.

Once I was outfitted, it was time to get into the boat. This was a skill in itself. I did a few warm-up exercises. Like bending my knees backwards. This is why gymnasts make very good kayakers.

Getting into the kayak is like stepping into a toilet and sliding your legs down the drain. Except you'd have slightly more room in a toilet.

Once we'd all mastered getting into the boat, we were ready to put-in.

Our first lesson was to learn the wet exit. The wet exit is a kayaking term that means
    "GET OUT OF THE BOAT AS FAST AS YOU CAN!"

Think about it. You're upside down in the water. Squashed into a boat. And your job is to get out.

Most people master this the first time they try because
a) they realize they have become fond of breathing, and
b) they'd like to live to try it again.

Sharon, a member of my group, was not completely comfortable with this exercise. Sharon flipped over in the water and immediately started thrashing around. She dog-paddled up for air, gasping "Help! Help! I'm drowning!" Then she disappeared underwater.

Gator looked annoyed. He pulled his **spray skirt** and exited his kayak. Then he WALKED over to where the woman was struggling. The water level was barely up to his knees!

Gator flipped her kayak upright. Sharon was gasping.

"The water isn't deep enough to drown," Gator grumbled with a big basset hound yawn. Sharon only gasped. This would

have been a good time for Sharon to pull out some donuts!

After our morning lesson, Gator felt we were ready for the white water. I didn't feel ready for anything. I only knew that I wasn't cut out to be a tadpole. And I thought a child's inflatable pool was a better idea than the rapids.

The river was plainly visible from the pond. But it seemed 100 miles away as I carried my kayak and paddle in the hot midday sun. Wearing a wet suit and a helmet didn't help.

I couldn't believe it. We were going on white water.

We entered the river. I was praying that my morning lessons would pay off.

We were in the rapids. But at this point, they were more like ripples. We bobbed quietly along.

Things were going pretty well until I got a cramp in my leg. How many other great adventurers suffered through this, I wondered? I felt helpless.

I tried shaking my leg. This just caused the nose of the boat to swerve to the right. The **hull** rocked violently.

The cramp persisted. I thought about abandoning ship to shake out my leg. Then up ahead, I saw white water. Huge rapids leapt through a canyon.

I felt excited. I felt eager. I felt sick. "Look at the size of those waves!" I exclaimed.

Gator had told us to stay in the main current of the river. To avoid the **strainers.** Why would giant stainless steel kitchen utensils be in the river, I wondered? Were they perched on the sides of the river? Catching everything in their path? Would I find leaves, logs, dead fish, and dead people caught in them?

Gator yelled, "Paddle hard through this!"

I glanced at Sharon. She was white with fear. Did I look as frightened as I felt?

I was paddling furiously. I looked up. Directly in my path

was a boulder. That's a pet peeve of mine. Boulders that sit right in the middle of the river and don't bother to move for anyone. Even beginning kayakers.

I dug my paddle into the water to steer a course around it. I guess I dug a little too hard. I spun 180 degrees. Now I was going down the river backwards.

This brings us to the Second Rule of Kayaking Safety.

Always secure your donuts in watertight bags.

When you do flip over, you'll want your donuts to stay warm and dry.

The actual flip happens really fast. For about five seconds, I didn't even notice what had happened.

Suddenly, I was underwater. It seemed like something was missing. What was it? I couldn't quite put my finger on it.

Then it hit me like a meteor. (Or was that my head slamming into a rock?) I knew what was missing. AIR!

I panicked. This is it, I thought. This is my coffin. They'll find me somewhere downstream, upside down. My body will decompose. I'll be fish food!

Then I came to my senses. I knew my body wouldn't decompose. The water was way too cold. I would die of hypothermia long before becoming fish food.

Somehow, I surfaced. My boat and paddle were rocking gently in an eddy. We'd become separated. They eddied out without me. The nerve!

I swam over to my kayak. The cockpit was filled with water, making it a little heavier. Before, I could hoist it with one arm. Now it was slightly heavier than an oil tanker.

How would I get the water out? I knelt down beside my

waterlogged boat. I looked at it thoughtfully, my chin in my hand.

I made a few weak attempts to pick it up. Then I got smart. I waited for the instructor to come and do it for me.

Back on the river, I felt a surge of power. I'd tackled the white water. I'd mastered the wet exit. There was nothing I couldn't face.

We came to an eddy. Gator suggested we try surfing a hole. He explained how it was done. First, you paddle upstream to a trough. This is where water rolls over a boulder.

You surf it by placing your kayak in the trough and paddling as needed. Gator demonstrated.

I realized, a little too late, not to be fooled when things look easy. It was Gator's job to make things look easy. That way, he hooked you into trying it.

I started paddling upstream. I paddled forever. Two hours at least. I glanced over at the shoreline. I hadn't moved more than two feet.

So I put my head down and paddled harder. I looked up to find myself in the middle of a boiling rapid. It wasn't where I wanted to be.

I tried to get out of it. But it was holding me. I was stuck. Just when I thought I'd never escape, the rapid flipped me over.

I wet exited. Swam to my boat. Looked at it thoughtfully. And waited for Gator to dump out the water. One thing for sure. I was getting lots of wet-exiting practice.

As we paddled slowly into an eddy by the kayak shop, I realized our lesson was over. Sharon lunged out of her boat and dove for dry land. Gator thanked us all for being such a great group. (He lied.)

A feeling of pride swept over me. I'd done it. I'd kayaked white water! I wanted to sing. I wanted to shout. I wanted a donut.

Chapter 4

"Window Shaded" in the Gorge

Charlie's dad, Wick Beavers, introduced Charlie to kayaking. It started when Charlie was in sixth grade.

Now Charlie was 15. Over the last three years, he'd spent good days on the river. And some not-so-good days.

Charlie hadn't really gotten into kayaking until a year ago. But it wasn't too long before he mastered the **Eskimo roll.** Then he started paddling daily. Eventually, he got his handroll down. After that, he was hooked.

This summer, Charlie had spent most of his time teaching kayaking. He worked for Backdoor Sports, a kayaking shop in Steamboat Springs, Colorado. He was the youngest instructor they had.

Charlie noticed that if his students weren't having fun, they'd tense up. So he tried to organize games for them. He'd ask what sports they played. Then he'd make a connection to kayaking.

Charlie liked teaching. But he also looked forward to doing his own kayaking. He liked surfing holes and playing on the

Yampa River that ran through town.

And now, he and his dad were taking a river trip. He'd had some great trips already this summer. Paddling the Blue River and Northgate Canyon. Each one had provided its own thrills.

But nothing like this trip. How great to be staying in Buena Vista, Colorado! Along the banks of the mighty Arkansas River.

Charlie was excited. There were so many great rapids on the Arkansas. And he planned on hitting most of them. Granite Canyon, Pine Creek, and The Numbers—one of the most difficult stretches of white water in the Rockies.

Eventually, they'd do Brown's Canyon. Charlie looked forward to that. The rapids there had several boulder piles. Challenging even to expert paddlers! Charlie had heard tales back in the shop. Now he couldn't wait to see it firsthand.

They'd been on the river one day already. Charlie was looking forward to five more days of warmth and white water.

Today, they were at the Royal Gorge. Another challenge.

Charlie's mom, Bonne, and a friend, Carl Boerski, were along also. Charlie and Carl were paddling kayaks. His mom and dad were in a raft.

The Gorge on the Arkansas was known for its big water and killer ender spots. It had one Class V rapid and several Class IV and IV+ rapids.

Charlie gazed at the brown sagebrush. He stared at the high canyon walls on the side of the river. He floated along peacefully. Someday he'd really like to kayak the Grand Canyon—the ultimate kayaking experience.

The warm August sun felt good on Charlie's face. But his **dry suit** was getting hot. So he didn't mind the occasional splash of cold water against his skin.

Carl was behind Charlie. Charlie's mom and dad were farther back.

Charlie and his dad had shared many good times on the river. Like last Easter. That morning, he and his father had gone skiing. Then later in the afternoon, they'd paddled down the Yampa River.

So far, this morning had been great. Lots of fast water. Some great surfing waves. He and Carl had played on a few, doing **pop-ups, enders,** and **retendos.**

Up ahead, Charlie noticed the faint pounding of rushing rapids. Good, he thought. Some action.

Charlie handled his Perception Dancer XS with ease. It was a small boat and fairly old. He'd had it for two years. And by now, it had become almost a part of him.

Charlie was nearing the rapid. He could hear the grumbling jaws of the river. This was going to be trickier than he'd thought.

Charlie paddled hard into the hole. The blue sky vanished. Water came hurtling at his head. It seemed as if the rapids were caving in on him. All he could see was darkness.

Then, for an instant, the sky appeared again. Charlie sucked in for air. Then darkness.

Charlie had lost control, and the river had taken over. Its heavy paws were taking his kayak. Tossing it around like a toy.

Charlie flew forward into the cold water. Then in the same split second, he was up again. Forward. Down. Under. Up. Forward. Down. Under. Up.

Charlie and his boat were being cartwheeled in the raging rapid. And Charlie could do little at this point to stop it. The brown, foaming water was churning around him.

He tried to do the Eskimo roll. But the river was jerking his paddle every which way.

Finally, the rapid spit him out into calm water. It seemed like he'd been trapped for hours!

He hadn't really been scared. He hadn't had time. Now, it took only a moment for Charlie to realize what he'd been through. He was tired, and his body ached. It felt like he'd just been in an avalanche.

Charlie carved into an eddy and turned to watch the others. Carl put his head down and paddled hard into the rapid. His boat paused for a moment in the boiling water. All the while, his arms continued to paddle forward furiously. Then Carl's kayak jerked up slightly before passing over the edge of the hole. He eddied out alongside Charlie.

"Looks like you had a little bit of trouble," Carl said, breathing heavily.

"Yeah. I got **window shaded,**" Charlie said with a laugh. They both turned to watch Charlie's parents rock easily through the hole.

Charlie turned and looked downstream. Already, he was excited for more of that Arkansas River action.

Chapter 5

Terror at Cross Mountain Canyon

Tom watched his girlfriend Sandy. She was surfing a gorgeous blue wave called Dream Weaver. Its 30-foot face allowed two boats to easily glide over the glassy surface.

Sandy and Tom were in a beautiful spot on the Yampa River in Cross Mountain Canyon. This was the start of their three-mile kayaking trip. Three other friends—Calvin, Bo, and Don—were with them.

Tom looked downstream. He knew this would be a challenging trip. And this was just the beginning.

Recent floods had made the water level much higher than normal. Trees and debris rushed by in the foamy river. Each person was quietly nervous about what lay ahead.

The five decided it was time to paddle on. They peeled out into the main current of the river.

Just 100 yards ahead was the Osterizer. One of the worst rapids in the canyon. Here the river straddled a house-sized rock.

The five adventurers parked their kayaks in an eddy. Then they walked up to inspect the rapid.

On one side, the river dropped into a boiling hole. On the other side, there was a narrow chute called the Sneak.

Tom stared. How could a kayak fit between the boulder and the canyon wall, he wondered. It was such a narrow gap.

About this time, a large, telephone-pole-sized log approached. The huge log sliced through the Sneak.

Tom took this as a good sign. He was ready to try it himself.

Tom slid into his kayak. Then he peeled out into the fast-moving water. He focused on the challenge just ahead.

Tom paddled hard. Suddenly, he was in it. Just like the log, Tom squeezed cleanly through the Osterizer.

In minutes, the others had covered his same path. They were all through the narrow gully.

The next 3/4 mile was continuous Class V rapids. Coming out of the kayak would be life threatening, if not fatal.

But all five were expert kayakers who'd been paddling for years. They knew how to read the river. And how to control their fear. Or how to use it to their advantage.

The river roared. Brown water exploded through the canyon. Rooster tail sprays shot above boulders. The five paddled hard.

Each person was alert. Looking out for his or her own safety. At last, they were out of that stretch. But one wicked rapid after another followed.

The Labyrinth was the next big rapid. Tom peeled out of the eddy and headed for the rapid. Trusting him, Bo and Don followed.

Tom led them all right into a hole. All three were tossed

about. Finally, they managed to get out. "I'm not following you anymore," Bo declared.

On either side of them, sloping canyon walls were strewn with broken-up rocks. The river was a churning mass of brown foam.

Next, they paddled down to the Snake Pit. There they had to **ferry** to avoid slamming into a debris pile.

Then came the Slot. Here the waves were as big as the ones in the Grand Canyon.

The worst section of the river was now behind them. They pulled into a flat, sandy area. The kayakers cheered and slapped one another on the back.

"Didn't you feel like a leaf?"

"Did you see that in the Labyrinth?"

"I couldn't believe we were in there together."

"What about the Osterizer?"

"That was a little tight." Spirits were soaring.

At a beautiful beach just above Pour Over City, they had lunch. Tom glanced across the river to the opposite shore. No bighorn sheep today. Tom had seen one there many times. It seemed to be the ram's favorite watering spot.

Tom finished eating. He got into his kayak to paddle downstream. The others were still finishing lunch.

Normally, Tom would have waited for the others. His friends would have been waiting downstream with throw bags and ropes for backup. In case Tom needed help.

But not this time. Tom and the others weren't worried. Hadn't they done the worst part of the river? And Tom had done this section a couple of days earlier.

Pour Over City was loaded with car-sized boulders. So Tom decided to take the rapid **river left.**

He ferried out. The waves were huge. Ocean waves.

Suddenly, Tom was in the trough of a wave. All he could see was water above and around him. Until he crested the wave. Then he could see downstream.

He crested the last wave. He was looking down into a hole he hadn't seen two days earlier. The hole was huge!

Then it came to him. The wet conditions over the last 48 hours had changed the river. The water level had risen.

Tom knew only one thing to do. He put his head down and paddled as hard as he could.

The hole engulfed him. It whipped him around like juice in a blender. Tom screamed. He paddled furiously, his arms thrashing forward.

Ahead. The crest. He paddled hard. He had to get over it.

He neared the crest. He was just about over it when the water pulled him back and swallowed him again.

On the shore, the others watched. They knew he was in trouble. Sandy rushed to her boat and paddled out hard.

Meanwhile, Tom fought hard to exit the hole. "I'd think it was letting me go," he later said. "And then it would pull me back. Seconds felt like hours. Hours felt like days."

Tom was completely disoriented. Still, he fought hard.

He couldn't get over the crest. So he paddled straight down. He did an ender. This blew him and his boat out of the back of the monstrous hole.

At last, Tom was clear of the hole. But he was upside down.

He quickly rolled upright, only to face another challenge. He fell into the biggest pour over in Pour Over City rapid. The rapid pressed him down onto the river floor.

In most rapids, water rolls over a boulder. Then it hits the river bottom and circles back up. Objects or people caught in these types of rapids get spit out.

But Tom was caught on the bottom. Water was passing through undercut rocks below him. They were acting as a strainer. Pressing him harder into the rocky floor.

Tom felt nailed to the rocky floor. The boat hammered against the rocks. It was dark, black, and cold.

Tom had held his breath for as long as he could. Finally, he

had to open his mouth. Water rushed in. He gagged. He was choking. A burning sensation filled his head.

Was he going to die? No! Not that! He wasn't ready!

Tom saw the light of the river surface above him. If I can just get out of my boat, he thought.

He tore at his spray skirt. The water from the falls was pressing against him. Finally, he pushed out of his boat and popped to the surface.

He was still in the thunderous rapid. But now he didn't have a kayak or a paddle. His body was being hurtled down the river. His spray jacket was full of water.

Then he saw Sandy. She was in her boat trying to get close enough to save him.

Something hit him in the head. It was his boat. It had surfaced.

Tom grabbed it and hung on for his life. Then another rapid took control. Tom lost his hold on the boat.

Sandy was in trouble too. So she made the move from rescue to survival. That's an important rule of water safety.

At this point, Tom was only semiconscious. Feet over head over feet he flipped in the cold water. His chest burned.

He saw a boulder up ahead. He threw his arm around it and clung. Dry, he thought. It's dry!

With his last bit of strength, Tom crawled onto the boulder and collapsed. Then he passed out.

Tom awoke with a pounding headache. He started vomiting and couldn't stop. He had never felt so tired in his life!

Tom's friends were so relieved. They had caught up with him.

Tom was finally on dry ground. But he was on the wrong side of the river! Somehow, he had to get to the other side.

Tom's friends sat on the side of the river in their kayaks. Calvin offered Tom his kayak.

"I'll just hitch a ride by grabbing on to the **stern**" Tom said. "You can ferry me across."

Tom wasn't ready to get back into the water. But he knew he had to.

Tom grabbed on to the strap on the stern. Calvin started paddling for the other shoreline. But the river was too powerful. It took them right into another rapid.

Tom let go of the boat. Once again, he was knocked around. Tossed over and under until his head swam.

At last, he made it to shore. Tom crawled onto the bank and kissed the ground.

Tom had survived auto accidents, avalanches, and a hang

glider crash. But this was the closest he'd come to death. He'd lost his kayak, his paddle, and almost his life.

For days, Tom still had water coming up. His ears popped and his sinuses drained.

And by then, Tom realized his mistake. He had gotten too content. Too confident.

"I thought the worst was over," Tom said. "I let down my guard. I never should have done that."

It was a couple of days before Tom felt comfortable kayaking. He paddled some slow water. Just to get his nerve back.

A week later, he and his friends went to Dinosaur National Monument. They planned to paddle a section of river there.

The park ranger was checking their equipment. Tom mentioned that he'd lost a boat a week earlier.

"You lost a boat? What color was it?" asked the park ranger.

"Purple," Tom said.

"We found it."

"You're kidding! Where?"

The park ranger explained. Tom's boat had been found 70 miles downstream from where he'd lost it!

Eventually, Tom returned to Pour Over City. But not right away.

The river was lower this trip. And this time he stayed with the group. He didn't go off exploring on his own. He never let down his guard again.

Chapter 6

Kayaking Competitions

Kayaking competition is a growing sport. Many young kayakers have surged onto the white-water scene recently. Teenage paddlers from across the country are stunning judges. They perform amazing moves in boiling rapids. They show strong, precise control through slalom gates.

Summer river festivals are common in many towns. All festivals include a variety of events. Two common events are slalom racing and white-water rodeo.

Slalom racing demands complete control of a kayak. And split-second decision making.

Racers go downstream through a series of 25 gates. Gates are suspended from wires running across the river. They are about four feet wide.

Kayakers must pass through each gate in the proper order. And they can't touch them. Five seconds is added to a paddler's time for touching a gate. Fifty seconds is added for a missed gate.

The main event in the white-water rodeo is the freestyle.

This is sometimes referred to as the "hot-dog" event. This event features kayakers who paddle into a hole. They do spins, enders, retendos, and surfing.

White-water rodeo riding is hard work and tiring. Just like bull riding, competitors get bucked and tossed in the rapid. But rodeo riding is very rewarding for those who compete.

Glossary

cfs	(cubic feet per second) the measurement of water volume in rivers. 100–700 cfs is considered low volume. Over 3,000 cfs is considered high volume for most rivers.
Class I–VI	the rating system used to classify sections of rivers. Class I means slow moving water with few or no obstacles. Class VI is basically unrunnable.
dry bags	bags used to keep food and gear dry
dry suit	a suit that keeps you completely dry in the water
eddy	quiet spot in white water on the edge of a river or just downstream of a rock
eddying out	paddling from the river into an eddy
ender	a rodeo move in which the kayak stands vertically on its bow
Eskimo roll	the technique in which a kayaker underwater comes upright by sweeping the paddle back and snapping the hip at the same time
ferry	going from one side of the river to the other
handroll	rolling upright from an underwater position without the use of a paddle
hole	a trough formed by water flowing over a submerged rock
hull	the bottom of a boat
mesa	a flat area of rock that looks like a giant tabletop
peel out	a move done to leave an eddy and go downstream
pop-up	when the bow of the kayak is forced downward under the water and the end pops into the air
put-in	paddlers' lingo for the starting point of a trip

retendo	burying the bow of a kayak into the trough of a hole and then jumping up and down in the hole on the boat's nose
river left	paddling downstream, river left is on the kayaker's left side
river right	paddling downstream, river right is on the kayaker's right side
scullcap	tightly fitting hat worn under helmet for warmth
spray skirt	a plastic skirt that fits tightly around the kayaker and is attached with a band of elastic around the opening of the kayak. This keeps the water from spraying into the boat.
stern	the rear of the boat
strainers	anything in the river that allows water but not a body or boat to pass through. Trees and brush are two examples.
take out	paddlers' lingo for finishing point of a trip
throw bag	flotation device on a rope used to rescue kayakers in trouble
wet suit	a rubber jumpsuit that fills up with cold water. The water warms to your body temperature.
window shaded	kayaking lingo that means tossed around by a rapid